Rosamond Lehmann's
Album

ROSAMOND LEHMANN'S ALBUM

With an Introduction & Postscript

by Rosamond Lehmann

CHATTO & WINDUS
LONDON

Published in 1985 by
Chatto & Windus Ltd
40 William IV Street
London WC2N 4DF

British Library Cataloguing in Publication Data
Rosamond Lehmann's album.
1. Lehmann, Rosamund—Biography
2. Novelists, English—20th century—Biography
823'.912   PR6023.E42Z/
ISBN 0-7011-3004-0

Printed in Great Britain by
Butler & Tanner Ltd
Frome and London

Contents

Biographical Note

Rosamond Lehmann was born in February 1901, the daughter of Rudolph Chambers Lehmann, founder of *Granta*, editor and contributor to *Punch* and other journals, Liberal Member of Parliament, rowing blue and author, and Alice Davis, an American from New England. She was their second child. Her elder sister Helen was born in 1899, her younger sister was the distinguished actress Beatrix Lehmann, and her younger brother is the writer and editor John Lehmann. The family was brought up in a riverside house at Bourne End, Buckinghamshire, where the sisters were privately educated. In 1919 Rosamond Lehmann went to Girton College, Cambridge, where she met her first husband, Leslie Runciman, whom she married shortly after graduating in 1922. For some years they lived in Newcastle, where she wrote her first novel, *Dusty Answer* (1927). In 1928 she married the artist Wogan Philipps, by whom she had two children – Hugo, born in 1929, and Sally, born five years later. Following her second novel, *A Note in Music* (1930), the family moved to the village of Ipsden, Oxfordshire, where they remained until 1939, and where she wrote *Invitation to the Waltz* (1932) and its sequel *The Weather in the Streets* (1936).

During the War Rosamond Lehmann and her children lived in a cottage on the Berkshire Downs; she contributed stories to her brother's *New Writing* series (later collected as *The Gipsy's Baby* in 1946), and wrote *The Ballad and the Source* (1944). From 1946 to 1952 she lived in the village of Little Wittenham, on the Berkshire–Oxfordshire borders, before moving to London. In 1953 she published *The Echoing Grove*. Then in 1958 her daughter Sally died of poliomyelitis at the tragically early age of twenty-four, and Rosamond Lehmann wrote no more novels until *A Sea-Grape Tree* (1976), which brings together themes from *The Ballad and the Source* and her partial autobiography *The Swan in the Evening*, which was published in 1967.

Created CBE and a Fellow of the Royal Society of Literature in 1982, Rosamond Lehmann is a Vice-President of International Pen, Vice-President of the College of Psychic Studies, and a member of the Council of the Society of Authors. She has five grandchildren, two great-grandchildren, and divides her time between London and a house near Aldeburgh, Suffolk.

The risk of inner experience, the adventure of the Spirit, is alien to most human beings. The possibility that such experience might have psychic reality is anathema to them. All very well if it has at least 'historic' foundation, but *psychic*! Face to face with this question the patient often shows a profound contempt for the psychic.

C. J. Jung

The kernel of all jealousy is lack of love.

C. J. Jung

C'est un dur métier que d'être belle femme

Charles Baudelaire, 'Confessions', from *Les Fleurs du Mal*

Love once seemed kind as air
When the dewfall gleams.
Now he's another thing –
Naked light, oh hard to bear,
Too much discovering
With his noonday beams.

C. Day-Lewis, *Song (Air 'Dermott')*

I felt as if the laws of the universe no longer applied to me since I was outside the normal frame of experience. A biological no-nentity to be phased out ... and sometimes the anger of the underdog plotting bloody revolution, plotting revenge.

Anita Brookner, *Look at Me*

From the silence of Time
Time's silence borrow
In the heart of today
Is the Word of tomorrow
The builders of Joy
Are the children of sorrow

William Sharp (Fiona Macleod) - written at Glastonbury

Introduction

I have never kept a diary, and this I often regret, because of the black holes in memory that open with advancing years. From time to time I have noted down passages of verse or prose which seem, for one reason or another, to have preserved personal reverberations or an echo in my consciousness. I have put down a selection of these as a prelude to this book – probably my last appearance in print. But this is not an attempt at a commonplace book or an anthology. It was originally the idea of Carmen Callil of blessed Virago Press and Chatto & Windus, publishers of my first and last books, after I had shown her some of my ancient photographs and albums; and it was her assistant, my grandson Roland, whose photograph appears on another page, who sought out and collected what was available from various sources, with untiring industry and tact. A sort of keepsake album it is meant to be, a light-hearted affair, containing surprising reminders of my family in our infant days, but leading on to some of the images of the years of miscalled discretion. My own album seems to have ceased abruptly just before the Second World War, but I went on hoarding photographs and snapshots of family and friends. It is incomplete, of course, as a record of friendship, lacking many old and dear friends, such as Margaret Lane, Elizabeth Jenkins, or the late Sir William Walton, to name but a few, partly because this is the age of colour photography so that some of the most delightful of the latter-day images are perforce omitted from this book; also because so many of my nearest and dearest are no longer here, so that Roland's searches sometimes came, alas, to a dead end. The captions are not intended as potted biographies, only jottings. At times a sudden spurt of memory has flung up a voice, a gesture, speaking directly to me, and I have written it down. Sometimes the memories which surround the image have remained indefinite, amorphous, although their reality to me is clear and ever present: for instance, such characters as Carrington, David Garnett, and several others.

I would like to start this foreword with some lines written by Roland himself, at the age of seven; verses neatly typed out in solitude and silence on his mother's typewriter, and left without comment, then as later, on her desk. The poem is entitled 'Helping Words'.

help me.
and me.
me too.
don't forget me.
help me too.
please help me.
the ship has sunk help me please.
so has my ship sunk help me
too not only them please me too.

(Now the tone changes, becomes threatening, panic-stricken)

rescue me at once I demand you
too or i will tell the pliceman.
i'll do the same if you're not quick.
hurry up i'm drowning.
if you don't be quick i'll send you to court.

replys
yes i will
I am being as quick as I can.
all right I am coming.
you're not in all that of a hurry.

Several friends to whom I showed these remarkable lines felt that they might well refer to a distant memory of drowning in a former life. Be that as it may, I quote them because they define in starkest language serious emotional crises in universal human life: helplessness, a desperate plea for help from one moving about in worlds not realized, fear, impotent rage against the 'pliceman' Fate; *Rage, rage, against the dying of the light*, to quote Dylan Thomas's exhortation to his dying father (not a poem I care for); finally the appearance of the benevolent, venerable, archetypal sage himself, counselling patience and peace of mind. All is well. Stop fussing. Wait. Good advice indeed for an old person like myself.

I have written elsewhere of my own initiation into the world of words. I find now that it goes back even further than I thought. A bulky sheaf of foolscap has surfaced, headed, in my father's handwriting, *Rosie's Story, age five*. It begins in huge, 'joined up' script 'There was once a dog called Nelly, and her coat was as soft as silk'. Then the storyline rambles on rather drunkenly through dark woods, through the appearance of the Fairy Queen, emerging at last upon a sea shore, where Nelly declares 'I am weary of this life. Shoot me first, then I will shoot you. But what do you think happened?' At that point imagination must have failed me. My first letter has also been preserved, headed *Rosie, age six*.

Dear Mama,

The other day I bouhgt a Tom Tit pen. Helen liked it so much that she was mad about it, so I told her to shut her eyes and I hid it under a cushoin and she found it. Then we danced about like wild rabbits. Then we both tumled over together.

Your loving Rosie

Perhaps my account of that dramatic event does show a touch of talent? I have elsewhere recorded the creative surge that overwhelmed me in my first decade, but nothing from any deep, dark, unconscious level has appeared: it was all turned to favour and to prettiness. More like a bubbling forth of ectoplasm, or perhaps, more accurately, of those flimsy, faintly irridescent bubbles we used to produce and fling about the nursery from mugs of soapy water through clay pipes (the prototype perhaps of those emotional soap operas I later produced, according to one distinguished biographer?) What seems to me so curious in retrospect is that these reams of doggerel were always accompanied by disturbing physical symptoms – feverish heartbeats, stirrings and gripings in the bowel, as of one wrestling with strong signals from the unconscious.

But there is no malaise attached to what I am writing now. I feel a strange sense of freedom: of being – almost transparent, yet there is a residue of poignancy, of homesickness, for obvious reasons. Nothing to work out, to manipulate, to transmute or exorcize. When I examine these early scenes and images, I do in fact detect a world of concealed protagonists that coalesced much later, fractionally at least, into fictional material. But all is innocent; no beady-eyed prober is likely to spot or find a clue: though who is safe in this age of the new, post-Freudian criticism? I read lately in Michael Slater's masterly book *Dickens and Women* that Steerforth, that archetypal example of masculine glamour and treachery (not my *significantly* favourite Dickens character, by the way), was probably derived from his creator's agonising early love affair with the fickle Maria Beadnell. The psychological equations get more and more tortuous and arcane. What would Dickens, in those unenlightened days, have said to that suggestion? I expect he would have burst into 'a roar', meaning hearty Victorian laughter.

Lately I have been leafing through my works (rather reluctantly as always) to track down the obsessions which the very intelligent Gillian Tindall, in her *Rosamond Lehmann: An Appreciation* (1984), has so embarrassingly, if perhaps correctly, noted in my works; and I find that she has missed one: namely dogs. Dogs abound to an extraordinary degree in every story and novel. Why is that? Can it simply be because my childhood days were populated with them, because, like all his children, I have inherited my father's love of them? There were even portraits of several of the great and magnificent ones of former days in the boathouse, on the stairs and in the Servants' Hall. I dream that I shall wake up after death sitting in a branch of the walnut tree, watching my father open the French windows of the library, step down, and start strolling towards the river accompanied by two or three high-spirited dogs of varied breeds. But is there a psychological complex buried there – something much more disturbing? I have never felt altogether at home in the world, as if I had made some mistake before birth, in a previous incarnation, and could never put it right. As if my illustrious heritage, just out of reach in the world of art and letters and music, meant that I had inherited huge debts that I would never be able to pay. Or was it simply that poring over my father's memoirs I came upon this contribution from a contemporary of his grandparents:

I remember a little dance in Edinburgh at which Mrs Robert Chambers and one of her seven daughters [my grandmother perhaps] played the piano and the harmonium. Musicians will understand my surprise when I heard the daughter say to her mother 'Not in G, Mama, let's play it in A': whereupon they resumed the altered key (a difficult and intricate feat) as if it was the easiest and most natural attribute of the performance.

How I longed, with almost painful envy, to have been one of those of my great-grandfather Robert Chambers's incredibly talented daughters. Still, I continued wrapped in a cocoon of exceptional advantages: nurseries, schoolroom lessons, annual seaside and annual pantomime, birthday parties, the house filled with aunts, uncles, cousins, and constant delightful, kindly and talented weekend visitors – editors, writers, rowing blues, poets, politicians. Maybe the sense of threat I so clearly remember was simply the neurotic foreboding of a thin-skinned, introverted child, or maybe those of my generation – what is left of them – who remember the pre-1914 sheltered Edwardian world, have all felt outsiders ever since. It may account for the element of nostalgia in my novels, and their concentration on the individual's desire for love and fear of rejection, of death, of loss of love; also for their awareness of the breakdown of traditional hierarchies of the class into which I was born. Those were the days when critics of fiction still spoke of its moral influence and deplored the novels of 'emancipated young women' like myself.

In *The Swan in the Evening* I have already written of those things; it is the only one of my books I would like to be remembered by, and I think it possible I shall be because it contains an account of a direct experience of reality, mere glimpse though it was, that changed my life, and can never be formulated or anatomized or tampered with by those whose habit of mind produces 'contempt prior to investigation'. In any case, apart from the vast, unshakable consolation, the extension of intellectual and spiritual knowledge, it helped to bring some of the most precious friendships of my life.

I never knew my grandmother – alas – she died when I was two. But I used to read, and re-read – I still do – her letters to my grandfather, privately printed by my father after the former's death, with an extraordinarily intense feeling of identification with her – her kind of temperament, her passionate love of family and friends, her acute sense of the heart and of the ridiculous. She must have had a talent amounting to genius for friendship, as well as for music. And when on my twelfth birthday I was given her little engagement ring – a half hoop of small cut rubies set in gold – it seemed to reinforce my hitherto immaterial sense of being linked with her, and with her far off, ever-present world in which friendship, lavishly given and received, seemed to be the predominating, stabilising element. Strangely, now that I am old, this element has strengthened rather than receded.

Robert Browning said once, when being congratulated on his happy, fortunate life, 'Yes, but when I look back, it seems to be mostly pain'. I know very well what he meant, yet at the same time the backward look shows me a personal landscape glowing with serenity and loving kindness. Its precariousness seems overlaid by a mantle spread by goodly creatures. When I look at the hundreds and hundreds of letters I have preserved, I see, with inexpressible gratitude, how richly I have been accompanied, supported, cherished, by my friends. So I repeat, this album is a simple, sketchy record of a life, at least in one sense exceptionally fortunate. If being an insider means being deeply, irrevocably sunk in the human condition, one with the humbler creation, hoping to keep on the side of the true angels, then I have become a true blue insider. I dedicate this album to my son, my five grandchildren, and my two great-grandchildren. They all appear to me marvels of seemliness on every level. Reader, farewell.

The Album

An early photograph of my adored father R. C. Lehmann – scholar, athlete, editor, author, Member of Parliament.

My mother, Alice Marie Davis.

Fieldhead, Bourne End, Buckinghamshire, the
house built by my father where we were all
born and brought up. I describe it and the
garden and my passion for it in *The Swan in
the Evening*.

The first picture of me, February 1901 – my
mother wears a melancholy expression. She
had hoped for a son.

Helen, my father and myself. My father taught us all to swim, also to punt and feather our oars when we sculled. Highlights of the river days were when the Oxford or Cambridge crews (coached by my father) came to stay – the god-like rowing blues I describe in *The Swan in the Evening*.

With Helen.

The schoolhouse my father built for us in the garden, designed by George Drinkwater. I started my education here at the age of four with Helen and our little neighbours Thelma, Delphine, Norah and Enid, under the tender care of the beloved Miss Davis, who so cheered me when I was worried about my status as the middle child of the family: 'I'm the middle one too, in my family. I think it's rather nice. Like the jam in the middle of the sandwich.' After her departure the school was taken over by two unforgettable spinsters, Miss Edwards and Miss Winson, and continued to expand and flourish. I enjoyed an inadequate education here until I went to Girton at the age of seventeen.

With my sisters Helen and Beatrix and my brother John in 1907: in those days he and I were the apple of one another's eye. He figures in *Invitation to the Waltz*.

My mother with Helen, Beatrix and myself.

A gloomy group of bridesmaids and a page, decked out for a cousin's wedding in 1913.

These family groups were taken from time
to time to send to my mother's mother in
New England.

My mother produced a charming nativity
play, *Holy Night*, during the Great War. My
brother wore the costume of a cock who at
one moment crowed. Talented local ladies
were busy making wings, and our footman
remarked 'Miss Rosie looked well as an angel'.

This was taken during the Great War, when my sisters and I used to help at a neighbouring home for blinded officers. My mother thought this an acceptable contribution to the war effort – but it proved a more enlightening experience than she realised. Very moving too.

Siegfried Sassoon and his wife – he was a favourite (First) War-time hero of Beatrix and myself. I saw him quite often during the Thirties.

In the summer before the Great War we
went to Chateau d'Oex in Switzerland for
our holidays. Helen won this race – I came
second.

Taken shortly before I went to Girton, with
another beloved dog.

Setting off for a picnic from Girton.

My first husband, Leslie Runciman, with a horrible little dog from Battersea Dogs' Home, mistakenly selected by myself.

George (Dadie) Rylands – 'onlie begetter' of my career as a published novelist. This is the first recorded image of a life-long friendship: I had just finished *Dusty Answer* and nervously suggested he should read it. He nobly consented and, what is more, sent it to Harold Raymond of Chatto & Windus with a letter of recommendation. So it was he who started the whole thing. He is on the right of this picture.

ST-WAR
LEM.

eparations." By Carl
Foreword by Sir Josiah
.B.A. (Benn. 21s.)

HILIP MORRELL.

his new edition of Herr
n book on reparations
tune. "The present
sh Stamp writes in his
n, "is one of calm. . . .
taken the problem of
, of the political sphere
conomic field." A great
attended by 350 dele-
he civilised countries, is
va. What better time,
en chosen for publishing
of the history of that
which for over nine years
the best minds of Europe
not yet finally solved?

principle of reparations
serious dispute. "Com-
made by Germany for all
s civilian population of the
property by the aggression
and, by sea, and from the
he declaration before the signing
five days before the signing
But to enunciate a principle
aborate it, to interpret it,
other, as Europe, through
rish tension, amidst infla-
tent and misery, was to

NEW FICTION.

A REMARKABLE FIRST NOVEL.

"Dusty Answer." By Rosamond Lehmann.
(Chatto and Windus. 7s. 6d.)

This is a remarkable book. It is not often
that one can say with confidence of a first novel
by a young writer that it reveals new possibilities for literature. But there are qualities in
this book that mark it out as quite the most
striking first novel of this generation. The
title, of course, is taken from George Mere-
dith's "Modern Love":—

Ah, what a dusty answer gets the soul
When hot for certainties in this our life!

But the book itself is a study of modern youth,
and its outlook is entirely that of the present
day. It traces the development of the character of its heroine—Judith—from childhood,
with her childhood's companions, and through
her career at Cambridge, with its friendships,
and the emotional snare in which Judith's first
love struggles like a young falcon for truth.
The modern young woman, with all her frank-
ness and perplexities in the semi-pagan world
of to-day, has never been depicted with more
honesty, or with a more exquisite art. The
word "exquisite" is not used lightly here.
The style is lucid and simple, and it has the
subtlety of those great qualities. It is the
kind of novel that might have been written
by Keats if Keats had been a young novelist
of to-day. Take, for instance, this quite
casual bit of description (of an afternoon in
the summer term at Cambridge), with its
clour and atmosphere:—

A review of *Dusty Answer* by Alfred Noyes.
The first couple of reviews I saw gave the
impression that I had gravely offended
against standards of womanly decorum. I
wished the earth to open and swallow me
up. But then, after that first upsetting week,
a long article by Alfred Noyes appeared in
the *Sunday Times* – and, all at once,
bewilderingly, the book took off, had rave
notices, became a best-seller. In France the
object of a kind of cult, Book of the Month
in the USA, hundreds of letters pouring in
from strangers . . .

" Dreadfully," sighed Mrs. Debenham. " But supposing a girl does marry for money—after years of poverty, as Kitty did—you wouldn't give her a chance ? "

ives for
e was a

she knew

e," he went
; Pelew case

i quietly.
n with no
the future.
the man of
ns solemnly

ssarily harsh
t quiet voice

" I extracted

" You were
n't have been
....with any

long time.
ve years !"
in five min-
i a different
i your brain
er, to make

" A chance for what ? "
" Happiness....romance...."
" A woman who marries for money and gets money, should stick to her bargain instead of keeping up an elaborate pretence of doing so. There is no common honesty in such women."
" No. I suppose not. It's rather cold up here."

  * * *

He was waiting in the lounge when she came down the following morning.
" Sleep well ? " he asked.
" Splendidly. I always do."
" There is an old Roman wall I thought you would like to see," he said.
" Why ? " she asked.
" It's....it's incredibly old."
" No, thanks. I want a chat with you, Forbes. About Mrs. Pelew this morning. I've been thinking about Kitty this morning. I told you I was fond of her."
" Yes," he said, and he watched

ither-in-law, Sir Louis Kershaw, ot
India Office, were all there.

Yevonde

Mrs. Leslie Runciman

Mr. Walter Runciman's daughter-in-law, who has just published, under her maiden name of Rosamond Lehmann, an exceedingly clever first novel " Dusty Answer"

Book of the Month

Every time the news reaches England of the choice of the " book of the month " in America—last month Miss Rosamond Lehmann's " Dusty Answer," a first novel, was chosen with 45,000 votes in a club which specialises in this sort of thing — one hears talk of the possibilities of such a club being organised over here.

The more independently-minded readers are against " spoon-feeding "

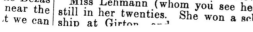

of their literary fare, but the vote of a club of some 70,000 members does provide a certain criterion of choice for readers who do not consistently read reviews.

Miss Lehmann (whom you see here) is still in her twenties. She won a scholar ship at Girton, and

Consul-
was very
is Hind.
ids, both
and the

uch," said
ing talker
laughingly
not make

working
orld was
finished
he early

erful in
hat it is

he Bezas
near the
t we can

Christian,
ptiful, Mrs.
what

Riv
I
who
weat
The
says, i
In th
Mrs. Sc
madge,
people.
The bath.
tumes vie wit

From Fowl

The followi
wishing Mar
she opened
Calf " :
" Love ar
Am saving
bouquet f
killing th
Sam is
terrier.
cherished
summer
chickens
of his

One of the many who wrote me fan letters after *Dusty Answer* enclosed this photograph with her letter – 'I am a dancer . . . But only like this when melted by love and sun.' She was not the only one, male or female, to write in this vein.

A FORE-TASTE OF COWES WEEK.

MR. RUSSELL, MISS O. GUINNESS, MISS RUSSELL, MISS MAUREEN GUINNESS, AND MISS AILEEN GUINNESS

SENATORE AND THE CONTESSA MARCONI

COLONEL J. A. COLE AND MISS COLE

GENERAL THE RIGHT HON. J. E. B. SEELY

LORD AND LADY DORCHESTER

Given any sort of luck with the weather, Cowes this year promises to be something like a best ever, as entries are particularly and in one instance a bumper, for a short time ago it was reported they had fifty for the 14-ft. dinghy race for the Prince of Wales Cup, a new feature on the opening day, August 1. For the R.Y.S. programme they open with the King's Cup on August 1. All the big boats which have been racing in the Clyde will be on the premises. The Solent is already filling up and the Cowes Roads are full of yachts of all sorts and sizes. The group in the left-hand top corner is of some of the ship's company of *Fantome* taking a stretch its legs. Miss Oonagh Guinness and her sisters are the daughters of the Hon. Arthur Guinness, Lord Iveagh's brother. Miss Aileen Guinness' engagement to the Hon. Brinsley Plunket was announced last week. Senatore Marconi is with his bride, who was the Contessa Bezzi Scali. General the Rt. Hon. J. E. B. Seely never misses Cowes. He is Lord-Lieutenant of Hampshire. Colonel Cole and his daughter came ashore from the S.Y. *Cygne*, and Lord and Lady Dorchester are also some of Cowes floating population. Lord Dorchester has a house, Hamlet Lodge, in Cowes

More pictures from Cowes in this week's "Eve"

THE AUTHORESS OF "DUSTY ANSWER"

MRS. LESLIE RUNCIMAN

Who is a daughter-in-law of the Right Hon. Walter Runciman and the wife of Mr. Walter Leslie Runciman. Mrs. Leslie Runciman is the daughter of Mr. "Rudy" Lehmann, the great oar who has made so much rowing history, was captain of Leander, a Cambridge Blue, and in his more studious moments a great humorist and also the author of the Isthmian Library (Rowing) in his more serious mood. Mrs. Runciman's first novel, "Dusty Answer," has had a well-deserved success

Photographs by Yevonde, Victoria Street

Myself staying with my American Aunt on a visit to New Hampshire shortly after the publication of *Dusty Answer*.

Compton Mackenzie: he and John Galsworthy wrote me generous letters after the publication of *Dusty Answer* hailing me as a new star, Compton declaring 'my cloak has fallen upon you'. I could scarcely believe such a famous figure would take an interest in me; he became a close friend, and the godfather of my daughter Sally.

Grizel Hartley, whom I met at Girton. Oldest, dearest and best of friends, whitest of white witches, ineffable in hospitality and loving kindness. Once I said to her mother what a wonderful doctor she would have made (she had studied medicine at Cambridge): 'No, no,' said her mother, '*much* too much heart.'

With Wogan at the Mill House, Tidmarsh,
which I rented for summer of 1928. Lytton
and Carrington once lived there.

My former husband Wogan Philipps.

With Robert Gathorne-Hardy and Kyrle Leng at Stanford Dingley. Bob was one of my son Hugo's godfathers.

With Wogan and Dadie in Poitiers: the trip to French cathedrals we made in 1930 I describe in the *Letter to A Sister* published by Virginia and Leonard Woolf in The Hogarth Press series after my return.

Matt Ridley: I stayed with him and his wife Ursula a great deal at Blagdon and in France – he pretended he had collected all these bottles for me, the fantasy being that I had a passion for all liqueurs, the stickier the better.

At a fair in France, on the same holiday.

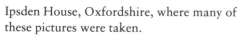
Ipsden House, Oxfordshire, where many of these pictures were taken.

Frances Partridge, the writer, a very dear friend for over fifty years now, staying at Ipsden in 1931.

Wystan Auden, Stephen Spender and Christopher Isherwood, who used to come over from Oxford to stay at Ipsden.

Stephen writing at Ipsden – I first met him shortly after my son Hugo's birth in 1929, and he was blazing in the firmament as Oxford's Young Poet. Ever since then he and his wife Natasha have been much-loved friends.

One of the writers with whom I often stayed was Rosamond Lehmann, whom I had met when I was an undergraduate. She had then the beautiful Ipsden House in the Chilterns, which had once belonged to Charles Reade, the novelist. It had a garden partly surrounded by a screen of trees, through gaps in which the whale-like grey-green Berkshire Downs could be seen. The house and garden sheltered by the old trees had their own closed-in atmosphere of lawns and paths and old brick walls, in which some windows survived from the Elizabethan period, in a Georgian facade. (Stephen Spender, *World Within World*, 1951)

John Banting, a true bohemian, lovable
eccentric, who designed surrealist murals at
Ipsden, as well as many of the Hogarth Press
jackets, with my dog Sheltie and E. B. C.
(Topsy) Lucas, the novelist, 1930.

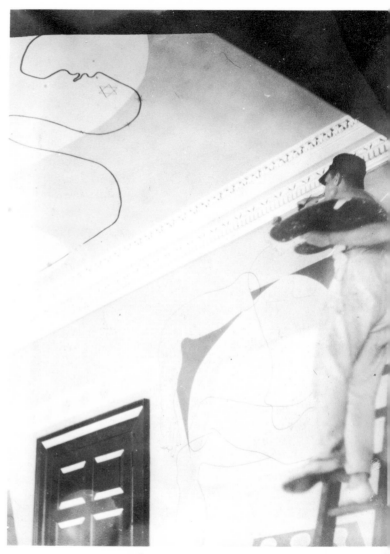

The murals being painted.

Carrington, who painted frescoes on the
nursery doors at Ipsden – I wonder if they
have survived.

Wogan and Lytton Strachey at Ham Spray, his home
where we were constant visitors up to the time
of his death. He and Carrington were dearly-loved
friends and neighbours when we were at Ipsden.

Lytton, Dadie and myself in the gardens of
King's College, Cambridge.

Eddie Sackville-West and Roger Senhouse.

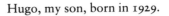
Hugo, my son, born in 1929.

The John family and Henry Lamb: Augustus John (absent here) once started a portrait of me, which later had to be abandoned. He and Wogan used to go pub-crawling together, until one night Wogan came in late, announcing that they must give up these trips, as it was bad for his health and he had started hallucinating. On the way home that day he had seen two elephants in the road. He was *so* worried that I promised to ring Augustus next day. I did, and carefully asked if they had had any strange experiences the evening before. 'No, no'. They hadn't seen anything odd in the road on the way home? No, nothing odd, only a couple of elephants. They were part of a circus on the move.

Henry Lamb also painted my portrait. I found the sittings unnerving; he scolded me for using lipstick. He talked obsessively, often bitterly, of Augustus. I remember his beautiful wife Pansy (Pakenham) with more affection.

Futility of Life Asserted With Skill; but Why?

Rosamond Lehmann

A NOTE IN MUSIC. By Rosamond Lehmann. 319 pp. (New York: Holt; $2.50.)

My second novel, was published in 1930.

With Ralph and Frances Partridge at Ipsden in 1931. Ralph was a remarkably gifted and original man, once married to Carrington. His massive masculine physique and cast of mind were balanced by an almost feminine intuitive sensibility. The youngest major in the army in 1914, he became a pacifist in World War II.

Ralph, Wogan and myself.

I can remember nothing about this strange picture, except that it was taken by Leonard Woolf.

Siegfried Sassoon sitting on the gate of a house near Salisbury which he rented for a time.

Princess Edmond (Winnie) de Polignac (on the right) in Paris; she introduced me to Cocteau (whose *Enfants Terribles* I later translated) and others at her famous salon in Paris. One person I met with her was Colette: she came in late one afternoon to have a chat with Winnie. She was wearing a shapeless dark voluminous garment and sandals on her bare feet. She took no notice of me, and talked about cooking; at one moment she looked at me and then murmured to Winnie: 'Je n'ai jamais vu un visage si bien fait' – which, as you can imagine, filled me with blushing surprise and delight.

When she got up to go she shook hands with me, smiling her wonderful smile, and said I must excuse her, she hadn't read my book (*Poussière* – the French title of *Dusty Answer*) and didn't suppose she would as she read no novels nowadays.

James Julian Alix

James Strachey, brother of Lytton, well-
known psychiatrist and translator of Freud,
Julian Bell and Alix Strachey at Ham Spray,
1930.

Stephen Tennant. When I was first married
and living in the North, my mother-in-law
organized a pageant at Alnwick Castle; I
played the demeaning role of a (male)
herald, with little to do except to run along
the battlements at one point, looking out for
the enemy. Stephen was to play a similar
part. As we sat in our rough male sackcloth
and cross garters awaiting our brief moment
of glory, we fell to discussing our favourite
colours. Blue, I said, then red. Then – pink.
'Oh, pink! I almost *faint* when I think of
pink.' Such was our laughter that we totally
missed our cue. I don't think we were
forgiven.

Julia Strachey, in a photograph taken by Lytton.

Hester Chapman at Ham Spray, staunchest and most generous of friends, but, if offended, implacable. A reckless and hilarious conversationalist, one aspect of her is brilliantly recorded in Frances Partridge's book *Julia*. An unfairly neglected historical biographer, she is here seen with Lytton, Stephen (Tommy) Tomlin, and Roger Senhouse.

With Ralph, Wogan, and Saxon Sydney-Turner.

BEATRIX LEHMANN

PHOTO BY ANGUS McBEAN

Beatrix, my younger sister – our yet unpublished letters to one another show our life-long closeness. I was with her when she died in 1979 and miss her always.

Vanessa Bell and Duncan Grant arriving to stay at Ipsden in the Thirties.

With David (Bunny) Garnett.

With my beloved Dandie Dinmont, Sheltie, at Kidlington, where we lived just before Hugo's birth. Frances Partridge once asked me whom I would save first in a fire, to which I am supposed to have answered, without hesitation, 'Sheltie, of course, then Hugo, then Wogan'. Sheltie, who had a wild streak, bit a neighbour's hand and was condemned, but rescued by Siegfried Sassoon, with whom he lived a long and happy life.

DANDIE DINMONT *terriers arriving from Kent in an omnibus for exhibition at Tattersall's show yesterday.*

Charles Lindbergh, the American aviator, first man to fly the Atlantic. He and his wife, the novelist Anne Morrow Lindbergh, came over for the day when they were staying in England in 1934 after the notorious kidnap and murder of their infant son. We felt honoured by such a visit. Here he is watching a swarm of bees with Wogan and Beatrix. I wrote about these bees in 'A Dream of Winter' a story now in *The Gipsy's Baby*.

Rosamond was one of the most beautiful women of her generation. Tall, and holding herself with a sense of her presence, her warmth and vitality prevented her from seeming coldly statuesque. She had almond-shaped eyes, a firm mouth which contradicted the impression of uncontrolled spontaneity given by her cheeks, which often blushed. Her manner was warm, impulsive, and yet like her mouth it concealed a cool self-control, and the egoism of the artist. At this age she seemed at the height of her beauty: yet when I look at photographs of her then it seems to me that her features were in fact too rounded, too girlish, and that years confirmed a sculptural quality which one felt then in her presence but which later showed in her features. So that she was one of those women in whom even greying hair was a kind of triumph, a fulfilment of maturity which her youth had promised.' (Stephen Spender, *World Within World*, 1951)

Outside the Prado with Wogan on a wooden
horse – a forgotten incident.

Stephen Tennant and Siegfried Sassoon.

Virginia and Leonard Woolf: Virginia was supposed to be formidable and unkind to aspiring novelists, but I never found her anything but delightfully stimulating and affectionate. I remember her tapping me on the shoulder at a party and saying, 'Remember, we won this for you' – meaning the freedom to discuss sex without inhibition in masculine society. I felt particularly at home with Leonard – I loved that voice and those sapphire-blue eyes that Angelica Garnett describes in *Deceived with Kindness*.

Sally.

Hugo and Sally.

John Hayward, the scholar and editor, who lived with T. S. Eliot for many years after the War. I first knew him at Cambridge, when he was still walking. Later he was a frequent visitor in his wheelchair. Sally never appeared to think there was anything strange in his appearance – they adored each other.

My brother John.

This photograph of Beatrix and myself was taken by Angus Wilson, a remarkable amateur photographer and gardener of genius.

This may look like the end of the world, but
was in fact a perfectly ordinary, rather
enjoyable picnic on the Berkshire Downs.

With John and Beatrix: I always feel it was sad for Helen, who was beautiful, intelligent and talented, not to be included.

Sally and Hugo in 1936. She adored him, and stung one day by his accusation that she had no sense of humour, she bought herself, out of her pocket money, a joke book. She learnt the jokes by heart, and he was soon begging her to stop making him laugh. Her humour was never criticized again.

Sally writing her novel, aged two: 'Does a book like mine need a condex, Mummy?'

Hugo, aged six – he insisted on going to bed
in this headdress, he loved it so much.

Wogan and his ambulance – setting off for
the International Brigade and the Spanish
Civil War, 1936.

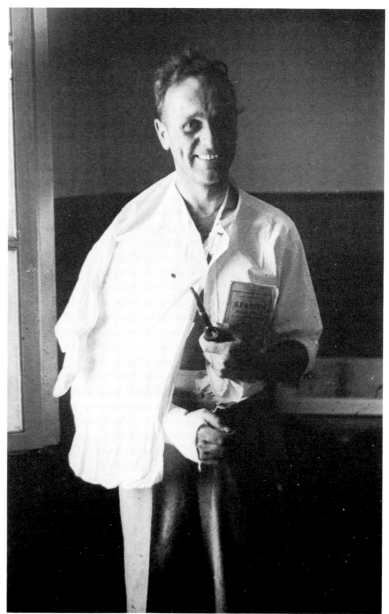

Wogan, after being wounded in the Spanish
Civil War.

Staying with Paul Cross in the West Indies, 1933.

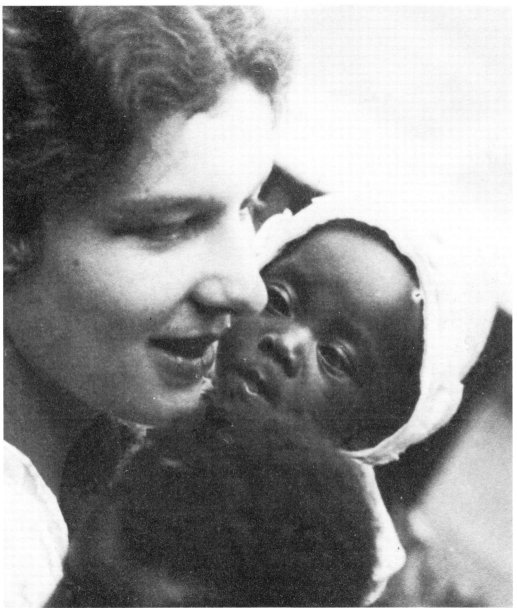

One of the babies I was offered in return for cosmetics – their parents said they had 'plenty more babies'.

With Paul Cross.

Performing a strange dance in the West Indies.

Beatrix, known to all her nephews and nieces as 'Auntie Peg', after a favourite pony who died when she was a child.

Beatrix with Betty-Ann Davis, Donald Pleasance, and a barely recognizable Alec Guinness in *Vicious Circle* by Jean-Paul Sartre at the Arts Theatre during the War.

Henry Green. Bizarre character. Melancholic. Author of *Living*, *Loving*, *Back*, and other brilliant novels. A fireman during the War, he allowed me to stay in his house in Rutland Gate, where he would come in streaked with dirt and exhaustion when off-duty, have a brief chat with me, and then go upstairs to write. He wrote to me once: 'These times are a wonderful bonus for us writers; in every crack and fissure of collapsing structures is lodged a seed of creativity.' In his case, this proved true.

Laurie Lee, who stayed with us for some months in my cottage on the Berkshire Downs in 1942, and was doted on by all, including Mrs Wickens, our housekeeper, who fortified him daily with her rice puddings.

William Plomer, the novelist, poet, librettist for Benjamin Britten, a constant visitor. His jokes and sympathy were unfailing. I visited him shortly before his tragic and untimely death in 1973.

Duncan Grant and Violet Hammersley; he painted frescoes and a portrait of her at her home in Totland Bay, on the Isle of Wight. They became devoted to one another. Violet was one of my mother's closest friends, and I spent many happy hours with her. There is a long description of her in *The Swan in the Evening*.

Bunny Garnett, in 1933.

Diana Gollancz, Victor Gollancz's daughter.

Raymond Mortimer.

Noël Coward: I was once extremely flattered
to hear him say in my presence –
'Extraordinary, I've never heard that woman
say a stupid thing'.

HAPPY CHRISTMAS
from
MASTER NOËL COWARD

Hugo.

Sally as a teenager: 'All the details I treasure of her beauty – the ravishing lines of her lips in smiling (the archaic smile – she really had it – its mysteriously subtle curve), her rather gliding walk, her odd slow buoyant grace when she danced, the something unforgettable about her eyes and eyelids – their extended outer corners, the grey-blue large iris flecked with green, the cut of the luminous lids, like segments of magnolia petal ... such images seem to set her in the antique world; in some golden age of plastic and poetic harmony, meaning, beauty; startling me now only a little more profoundly than they always did.' (*The Swan in the Evening*)

Sally Singing

Writing *The Echoing Grove*. I always write
first in longhand, and then re-write twice
more until it feels exactly right.

Cecil Day-Lewis, author of *The Lighted House*, *The Album*, and *An Italian Journey*, among many other poems. Also of the lines written on his tombstone, strangely enough part of a poem written for me and in my presence:

Shall I be gone long?
For ever and a day.
To whom there belong?
Ask the stone to say,
Ask my song.

AN
EXCERPT
FROM

THE
ECHOING
GROVE

a new novel by

ROSAMOND
LEHMANN

author of
four BOOK-CLUB SELECTIONS
ALL BEST-SELLERS

Joan Cross, a marvellous singer and a
marvellous friend, seen here as Mimi in *La
Bohème*.

Derek Hill, Heywood and Anne Hill:
Heywood and Anne are dearest of friends in
my Suffolk life.

Guy Burgess. He used to come to bathe in the river when we lived near the Thames. We discussed Victorian novels – he urged me to read Mrs Gaskell and *Middlemarch*. A stimulating friend. One time, however, he overstepped the mark, and expressed his hopes of seducing the gardener's handsome son. I forbade it. 'Oh, Rosie, Rosie,' he cried, '*can't* I?' 'No,' I said. This photograph shows him in Moscow and pains me by its expression of stress and torment. In earlier days he looked more like a cover for *Boy's Own Paper* – blue-eyed, pink-cheeked and curly-haired.

About to broadcast in Copenhagen, 1954.

In the early Fifties.

Duff and Diana Cooper: I was staying with them at Chantilly in 1952 when the telephone rang and they were told that Churchill had had a massive stroke, and would Duff please bring his obituary up to date. Diana wept. Duff stayed up all night. But Churchill recovered. I love and admire Diana, one of the last of our generation, who remains a magical beauty and brilliantly witty – I am proud to know her.

Bernard Berenson and Nicky Mariano. 'B.B.'
wrote to me after the publication of *The
Ballad and the Source*, saying that Mrs
Jardine seemed to him to be the portrait of
his late wife, and inviting me to stay (the
first of many times) at I Tatti. He hated, or
pretended to hate, all art historians, and
talked to me almost entirely about literature,
and other writers he had known, particularly
Edith Wharton. Once, speaking of Nicky
Mariano, he broke down, saying that 'she
should have had children'; he felt that she
was a born mother, and that he had
deprived her.

In 1951 with Julian Lezard: everybody's favourite dinner-guest, outrageous entertainer, reckless gambler and rider to hounds, and a one-time Wimbledon Champion tennis player. He became deeply involved in the famous 'Happy Valley' murder of Lord Errol, talked about it endlessly and fascinatingly, and had his own theory about the culprit.

T. S. Eliot, whom I knew after his marriage to Valerie in 1957. I admired and was very fond of him, and have remained devoted to her since his death.

Sally, at her wedding to Patrick (P. J.) Kavanagh.

Wogan and myself at Sally's wedding.

Laurens van der Post: citizen of the world. He lived through hell in Japanese prison camps and emerged to become a great spiritual thinker and writer. We meet at intervals and signal to each other. It was he who suggested the form for *The Swan in the Evening*, and who once said to me 'Trust your unhappiness, and great good will come to you, and greater freedom'. He was right.

Wellesley Tudor Pole: a great Seer, he founded the Chalice Well Trust at Glastonbury, where the antique and spiritually potent sapphire bowl he discovered in 1906 in St Bride's Well now reposes. I was his scribe, confidante and friend until his death in 1968, and he taught me most of what I know of metaphysics and the origins of Christianity. Author of *The Silent Road*, *A Man Seen Afar*, *Writing on the Ground*, and *Letters to Alexias*, his name for me.

Rose Macaulay: a marvellously witty writer, and one of my few unfailing comforters after Sally's death.

Robert Frost – a poet I had always much admired, and finally met on an unhappy lecture tour in America in 1958. All the audience wanted to knew was whether I had known Virginia Woolf. By great good fortune my lecture in Chicago was cancelled, and Robert and I were able to spend two days in happy communion, speaking of Edward Thomas and other poets. His charm was magical.

Elizabeth Bowen at Bowen's Court, County
Cork.

Goronwy Rees (the basis for Elizabeth
Bowen's Eddy in *Death of the Heart*) and
Stuart Hampshire during the same weekend,
known ever after as 'the Weekend where a
Great Deal Happened'.

Stephen Spender with his children Matthew
and Lizzie. A unique portrait of Stephen
with the face of a madonna – a Christmas
card from the early Fifties.

Angelica Garnett, daughter of Vanessa Bell, at Charleston in 1981. I used to watch her when she was a little girl, and try to imagine what it was like to be her, lovely, graceful, and surrounded by brilliance. There is a touch of her as Amanda in *The Weather in the Streets*.

Walter de la Mare. I was introduced to him only at the end of his long life (by Eleanor Farjeon), but it was as if we had known each other all our lives. After that he continued to send me his books of poems until he died.

My eldest grandchild, Anna, born in 1954.

My grandson Roland, the editor of this book, 1962.

With my eldest grandson, Guy, 1961.

My grand-daughter Kate, and my *great*-grandson Jack, 1982.

Jack with his sister Connie, the last of my late joys, 1983.

James Lees-Milne: best and most faithful
and amusing of correspondents.

Anita Brookner: of all the younger
generation known to me, the rarest in
quality both as friend and writer.

This is my last Testament.

What else is left that I might say?

I am in my eighty-first year, so it seems more than likely that this particular stage of my journey is drawing to a close. Once, the thought of living on through Time without Sally seemed too huge, too hopeless a burden to be borne; but nowadays, I seem to live partly out of Time: so that that lacerating illusion we create by having to deal life out in packets of days, months, years has largely disappeared. Time past, time present, time future are beginning to coalesce. I know that Eternity is not to come. We are in it here and now.

The start of my epilogue to the Virago Press edition of *The Swan in the Evening*.

Opening the Virago Bookshop, Covent Garden, in December 1984, with Carmen Callil, much-loved friend and publisher. To her I owe my 'Resurrection' as a novelist.

Postscript

My last novel was *A Sea-Grape Tree*, published in 1976, a sequel to *The Ballad and the Source*. I have, in my mind, a third novel in the sequence, which will now never be written, which draws together the threads of the first two books. But first, for those readers who may wish to be reminded of these novels, I shall attempt to reintroduce, briefly, some of the characters.

The Ballad and the Source spans the years of the Great War. The story unfolds through the eyes of Rebecca Landon, a ten-year-old, who lives with her family in the quiet of the English countryside. Through Rebecca we meet the scandalous Jardine family, who have returned to the country and live near the Landons: the enigmatic Sibyl, and her grandchildren Malcolm and Maisie (who is to become, for Rebecca, 'the first woman friend I ever had'). It is, however, Mrs Jardine who is the central character of the novel, a woman with a passionate, stormy past, who is to haunt Rebecca throughout her life.

Sixteen years later we encounter Rebecca again in *A Sea-Grape Tree*. Deserted by her un-named, married lover, she travels alone to a magical island in the Tropics. Here she meets Johnny who tells Rebecca that Sibyl Jardine is buried on the island. The other residents include Miss Stay, presiding genius and advanced psychic; Captain and Mrs (Ellie) Cunningham; Tony de Pas, the local plantation owner; Kit and Trevor, artistic lovers; and the once dashing Johnny, Mrs Jardine's last adored protégé, paralysed from the waist down in the First World War, his servant Louis, and his wife and nurse Jackie. Rebecca (or 'Anonyma' as she is known on the mysterious Isle) has a passionate affair with the reclusive Johnny, and as a token of his trust he gives her a medallion: inside is the address of the girl, Sylvia, he was to have married before his accident. Rebecca leaves the Isle with two promises: the first is to Miss Stay, to

care for her 'lamb', Ellie Cunningham, 'should occasion offer'; the second to Johnny, to pass the medallion to his former love should anything happen to him. But what echoes in her mind long after she leaves is neither of these two charges – it is the conversation she has had with the vibrant spirit of Mrs Jardine, who is still haunting the island and all its inhabitants. Her sinister shadow is finally lifted.

A Sea-Grape Tree is generally considered an unsatisfactory work. It would ill become me to argue for it; but perhaps I might just venture to say that Anonyma's conversation with Sibyl Jardine was intended to be a telepathic one. Telepathy between the incarnate and the discarnate is much less uncommon than is generally supposed. Sibyl is made to speak as she spoke on earth, as in *The Ballad and the Source*, in a somewhat didactic or mandarin style; but I see the experiment was rash and courted irritation, head-shaking, even mockery from a few critics ever willing and never afraid to wound. The action takes place on the brink, as it were, of another dimension, part poetic, out of time, part realistic: a kind of fabled or Prospero-type isle, where misfits, exiles in the world's terms, shipwrecked people, are washed up, find shelter, healing, loving kindness; even the dream of a love accepted and fulfilled. In her generous and beautiful introduction to the Virago Press edition, Janet Watts writes that the book requires a sequel. I did intend one. For the last time, I imagined, my 'daimon' descended, as of old, and drew back the curtain, showing me in one flash the entire landscape with figures, static, waiting to be animated, woven into an organic pattern. I saw it all; I knew it could be done, but the prospect daunted me, the energy required seemed altogether lacking. I have never in my life made a synopsis or sketched out a plot beforehand, but I do quite often think about this novel, seeing particular vignettes with clarity. This postscript gives a rough idea of this book that I shall never write.

The world of myth and magic is left behind for good; Anonyma resumes her name, Rebecca, and returns to 'ordinary life'. She goes back to the flat which she had shared part-time with her lover. She discovers the extraordinary reason why he failed to keep his date when she embarked for that tropic isle. The reason is quite clear in my mind, but I wish to keep it a secret. She breaks with him, and he disappears. Johnny writes that he will be with her exactly a year from now, but he does not come. It is now 1939. She hears, probably through Kit and Trevor, with whom she has kept in touch, the appalling news. Tragedy has struck the island. Tony de Pas has been murdered, found shot dead in his car. By whom? It is not known, but he had many enemies. Jackie, who loved him, is distraught. Johnny moves back to his own house on the hill, which he had left whilst having his affair with Rebecca, feeling that he cannot desert Jackie until she has recovered. After all, he married her, he says, and he is an honourable man. He says he will come as soon as he possibly can.

After that, months of silence from the Isle; and now it is September 1939. Rebecca has a compulsion to go in search of Maisie, and she finds her, running, perhaps, a maternity clinic in the East End, and it is from Maisie she hears the truth. Remember that Maisie (in *A Sea-Grape Tree*) was there when Sibyl Jardine died, and had made friends with all the community on the island. Johnny died in Louis' arms, without warning, of a heart attack. I don't see any of this clearly, but what is vivid is that Rebecca gets into her car and goes to somewhere in the West Country to return the medallion to Sylvia as she has promised. From the lane she watches Sylvia in the rather large garden of her thatched cottage, picking blackcurrants. I see exactly what Sylvia looks like – rather faded and untidy, nice face, wearing slacks. In the end Rebecca simply slips the medallion

through the flap of the letter-box and drives away. On the journey back it suddenly strikes her: 'But he knew he would never come back. He must have known even when he gave me the medallion'. War breaks out. She and Maisie have re-established their old intimacy and she agrees to take Tarni, Maisie's daughter, and perhaps one or two other children to her cottage in the country out of reach of the bombs. Tarni's father? Oh, Tarni is the fruit of a casual encounter on a walking tour, perhaps in France. 'I told you', said Maisie, 'I would never marry, but it doesn't mean I preserved my sacred virginity – not by a long chalk.'

Now comes Part II, and I think Rebecca writes it in the first person. This is mainly the story of Ellie Cunningham, whom she runs into by chance on a brief visit to London. Ellie has changed her name to Mrs Macleod, 'Mummy's name', has inherited a large, dreary London house from her only relative, an aunt, and has become an anxious, haggard landlady, keeping up soignée, lady-like appearances. She does fire watching. She takes lodgers, whom she distrusts, and finds 'very common, but you can't be too choosey'. But what has happened to her husband the Captain? 'Oh, he became totally infatuated with that awful nurse.' Told Ellie to clear out. 'It was sex,' says Ellie. Shortly after he had a massive stroke, and that was that. Rebecca recalls her promise to Miss Stay of the Isle, now passed on, to care for her lamb if she ever had occasion, and starts befriending Ellie, though with a sinking, uncharitable heart. Ellie has become more and more of a bore and a chatterbox; she has retained something of her pre-1914 appearance of a pretty woman ('She has much thicker hair than she used to have and the colour seems unreal. Can it be a wig?') She doesn't like dwelling on the past; it is too painful, but comforts herself with pious slogans. Sometimes Rebecca hears her murmuring 'God is kind'. She invites her to her cottage for the weekend, and Ellie and Tarni strike up a close schoolgirl friendship. They gossip together and garden, and wash their hair. Ellie teaches her to cut out and sew. Tarni has inherited much of her grandmother Sibyl Jardine's beauty, but *not* her character. She is a splendid girl – candid, stubborn, literal-minded, good as gold. After a couple of gin and tonics at the village pub Ellie bursts into tears, and out come all her woes. She has had hopes: her solicitor, a little younger of course, but not all that much, had obviously fancied her; taken her out to supper, gone home with her, made love to her. But she hadn't seen him since. Once or twice she rang up, and he always made excuses. But she's so lonely. She longs for a man in her life: she's a born homemaker, she says. Surely she has much to offer. 'There must be lots of lonely chappies, widowers retired from service abroad, still active and healthy – a gentleman, of course, it would have to be.' She's heard of a certain highly recommended Marriage Bureau. What does Rebecca think? Rebecca, of course, is only too happy to pay the quite stiff entrance fee. Hopes revived, Ellie has been introduced to a rather attractive, middle-aged bachelor, retired from the Indian Civil Service, so there is much in common.

Time passes – no word from Ellie. The telephone seems out of order, or is never answered. Finally Rebecca rings up the Marriage Bureau. 'I am sorry to tell you, my dear, that Mrs Macleod lied to us about her age. We cannot have *that* sort of thing. It would give us a bad name.' And where is she? They have no idea, she's no longer on their books. Next Rebecca hears that Ellie is in hospital. She goes to visit her, and finds her in a Jerry-built annexe of an evacuated hospital somewhere not too far away. At first she does not recognize her. She's deteriorating rapidly but still hopes that her friend the solicitor will pay her a visit – he has promised to do so. Tarni is very upset, she goes red in the face with angry, choked-back tears, when she hears that Ellie has died. 'She was nicer than, much nicer than – ' I waited ' – than almost anyone,' says Tarni. She insists on going to the funeral with Rebecca, carrying a huge bunch of flowers. Ellie is buried, by her request, beside 'Mummy', in a pleasant country churchyard. The only other mourner is the solicitor, a smooth-faced, old-young man wearing an old school tie. He has an opaque, cold eye. 'She was my mother's friend,' he says more than once, in case of any misunderstanding about her age and status in his eyes. Rebecca goes back to the hospital to collect poor Ellie's things which have been left to her, and a stout, plain, bespectacled nurse who had been kind to Ellie says 'She wandered sometimes near the end. They do, you know. She would keep on saying "Stay, stay" – something like that. Well, at first I thought she was on about her stays, or else she was wanting more of my attention, but I had plenty of other patients to see to. At the very end, about 3 a.m. one night, she opened her eyes wide, and gave such a smile and said that word again. "Stay", it sounded like.' (Ellie is seeing Miss Stay, Staycie, who has 'come to fetch her over' as she had promised, long ago.)

Most of this is taken straight from life, sad life. I knew the original of Ellie quite well during the War. She left me her only trinket, a little brooch. It has disappeared.

Acknowledgements

The publisher wishes to thank the following for their help:

The Camera Press (for the picture on p. 84)
The Hulton Picture Library (for the pictures on pp. 92, 97 and 100)
Tara Heinemann (for the picture on p. 106)
Elizabeth Winn (for the picture on p. 74)
A. D. Peters and Co. for permission to quote from *World Within World* by Stephen Spender

Laurie Sparham (for the picture on p. 105)
Sotheby's London, (for permission to reproduce the picture on p. 71 by Cecil Beaton)
James Lees-Milne, Stephen Spender, Angelica Garnett, Lady Selina Hastings, Barbara Ker-Seymer, Patchy Wheatley of BBC TV's *Bookmark*, Dr George Rylands, John Lehmann, Anne Norwich, Lady Anne Hill and particular thanks to Frances Partridge.

Index to photographs